THE BIG BOOK OF
Silly
DAD JOKES

THE BIG BOOK OF SiLLY DAD JOKES

750+ Jokes for Dads and Kids to Share!

CHRIS CATE

callisto publishing
an imprint of Sourcebooks

Copyright © 2025 by Callisto Publishing LLC
Cover and internal design © 2025 by Callisto Publishing LLC
Illustrations by Dylan Goldberger: cover
Getty Images: © doomko/iStock: ii; © lawangdesign/iStock: vi, 28; © seamartini/iStock: 3, 24
bottom, 79; © IgorZakowski/iStock: 6, 9, 12, 23, 59, 60, 74, 78, 86, 98, 125 left; © vostal/iStock: 8;
© ChuckWhelon/iStock: 11; © Easy_Company/Digital Vision Vectors: 14; © korobula/iStock: 15; ©
funwayillustration/iStock: 16; © yusak_p/iStock: 24 top; © Bayu Noviandi/iStock: 25; © lineartestpilot/
iStock: 26; © Tigatelu/iStock: 31; © andrewgenn/iStock: 36; © sararoom/iStock: 38, 49, 129; ©
shock77/iStock: 40, 76; © KenBenner/iStock: 43, 118, 120; © Jazzanna/iStock: 45; © memoangeles/
iStock: 46; © vostal/iStock: 48; © Cory Thoman: 50; © cako74/DigitalVision Vectors: 52; © larryrains/
iStock: 63, 84; © AntiMartina/iStock: 71; © Smokeyjo/iStock: 73; © lemonadeserenade/iStock: 75;
© azatvaleev/iStock: 80; © HitToon/iStock: 81; © Pavel Kostenko/iStock: 82; © den0909/iStock:
83; © carlacdesign/iStock: 87; © siridhata/iStock: 89; © ScottTalent/DigitalVision Vectors: 92; ©
memoangeles/iStock: 94; © ogieurvil/iStock: 96; © Lkeskinen/iStock: 100; © ourlifelooklikeballoon/
iStock: 102; © Cnuisin/iStock: 104 left; © abbydesign/iStock: 104 center; © FriendlyPixels/iStock: 104
right; © Roi and Roi/iStock: 105; © BluezAce/iStock: 110; © rivansyam/iStock: 114; © Bubert/iStock:
123; © MrAdvertising/iStock: 126; © colematt/iStock: 130
Shutterstock: © Gabi Wolf: 5; © TA Mulya: 7; © Shchasny: 17; © doddis77: 18; © Ken Benner: 20; ©
Elenor Design: 32; © pikepicture: 35; © HitToon: 56; © Marta Sher: 64; © sr-art studio: 66; © Buch and
Bee: 69; © Daria739: 90; © Alexander_P: 91; © innni: 93; © Sylverarts Vectors: 95; © Edyta.artdiary:
97; © Mark Rademaker: 99; © Victoria Sergeeva: 101; © hanec015: 103; © Back to Design: 108; ©
Mochipet: 125 right
Series Designer: Eric Pratt
Art Director: Angela Navarra
Art Producer: Stacey Stambaugh
Editor: Mo Mozuch
Production Editor: Rachel Taenzler
Production Manager: Martin Worthington

Callisto Kids and the colophon are registered trademarks of Callisto Publishing LLC.

All rights reserved. No part of this book may be reproduced in any form or by any electronic or
mechanical means including information storage and retrieval systems—except in the case of brief
quotations embodied in critical articles or reviews—without permission in writing from its publisher,
Sourcebooks LLC.

This book is a work of humor and intended for entertainment purposes only.

Published by Callisto Publishing LLC C/O Sourcebooks LLC
P.O. Box 4410, Naperville, Illinois 60567-4410
(630) 961-3900
callistopublishing.com

Library of Congress Cataloging-in-Publication Data is on file with the publisher.

This product conforms to all applicable CPSC and CPSIA standards.

Source of Production: Wing King Tong Paper Products Co. Ltd. Shenzhen, Guangdong Province, China
Date of Production: December 2024
Run Number: 5044371

Printed and bound in China.
WKT 10 9 8 7 6 5 4 3 2 1

Contents

The Setup		1
1	Hi Hungry, I'm Dad	4
2	Knock Yourself Out	42
3	Punny Because It's True	70
4	A Riddle Bit More	88
5	Stories You Can Tell...Are Jokes	106
6	Just for Kids: The Next Generation of Comedians	132

The Setup

The secret is out. You don't have to be a dad to love and tell dad jokes. They're for everybody, except skeletons who don't have *the guts* to tell dad jokes.

No matter what you're doing or how you're feeling, there's a dad joke for you. Don't believe me? I'll prove it.

You: "I'm doubtful you can prove it."
Dad: "Hi, Doubtful. Nice to meet you."
You: "You proved it. I'm impressed."
Dad: "Hi, Impressed. Nice to meet you."
You: "Okay, I'm leaving."
Dad: "Hi, Leaving. Where are you going? The best part of the book hasn't started yet!"

If these jokes sound familiar, your dad or granddad probably tells similar jokes when you're bored, scared, and/or hungry. That's the beauty of dad jokes. They're lighthearted, silly, and universally shared by dads over and over again. Even when dad jokes aren't laugh-out-loud funny, they're still fun. Groans and eye rolls are part of the mystique. Dad jokes can be so bad they're good.

The best dad jokes are passed down from one generation to the next like family heirlooms, which is why I can't claim to have written every joke in this book. In fact, you may have heard different versions of these jokes in your house. For instance, when your dad jokes about skeletons, he probably doesn't mention they lack the guts to tell dad jokes. He probably jokes about skeletons who don't have the guts for skydiving, boxing, or going to scary movies. Either way, skeletons have no body to blame but the simple and timeless dad joke structure we all love:

Obvious Setup + Cheesy Punch Line = Dad Joke

There are more than 750 dad jokes in this book. They're fun to read, but they're even better when you say them out loud. So, I encourage you to keep the tradition of telling dad jokes alive by sharing these dad jokes and creating your own variations for your family and friends. After all, whether you're a dad, mom, or kid—doubtful, impressed, or leaving—dad jokes are for everybody, except skeletons...and eggs who don't want to crack each other up.

Buckle up buttercup, we're just getting started. Let the dad jokes begin!

Hi Hungry, I'm Dad

Dad Jokes Are Popular, Apparently

Dad jokes have been entertaining families long before they were an internet fad. When the first kid on Earth asked, "Do you know how long dinosaurs lived?" the first dad responded, "Same as the short ones." And it wasn't his first or best dad joke that day. But don't let the name fool you. Dad jokes can come from anybody, anywhere, anytime—like right now:

When does a joke become a dad joke?
When it becomes apparent.

Don't overthink what makes a dad joke special! This opening chapter features tons of classic Q&A-style dad jokes. The setups are short. The punch lines are sweet. When it's all done, it'll be *apparent* why dad jokes are so funny and timeless, even when they deserve more eye rolls than belly laughs.

What is a snake's favorite subject in school?

Hisssssstory!

Do you know how heavy the sun is?
Me neither, but it's pretty light!

Where do hamburgers go to dance?
The meat-ball!

What day of the week are most twins born?
Twos-days!

How do you know the ocean is friendly?
It waves!

Why was the man running around his bed?
To catch up on sleep!

Why did the internet need glasses?
To improve its web-sight!

What kind of band can't play music?
A rubber band!

What does a cat say when you step on its tail?
"Mee-ouch!"

What did the Dalmatian say after lunch?
"That hit the spot!"

Why was the math book unhappy?
Because it had too many problems!

What kind of table doesn't have any legs?
A multiplication table!

6

What do you call a boo-boo on a T-Rex?
A dino-*sore*!

What did the triangle say to the circle?
"You're pointless!"

How do you make an egg roll?
You push it!

What do you always get for your birthday?
Older!

What do snowmen call their kids?
Chill-dren!

How did the Vikings send secret messages?
Norse code!

What is the longest word in the world?
"Smiles." Because there's a mile between its first and last letters!

What did the drummer name his two daughters?
Anna One. Anna Two!

When should athletes wear armor?
When they play knight games!

Why are skeletons happy?

Because nothing gets under their skin!

What did the bologna say to the salami?

"Nice to *meat* you!"

Why is everyone tired on April 1?

Because we finished a long 31-day *March*!

Why didn't the girl trust the ocean?

There was something fishy about it!

What do you call a turkey after Thanksgiving?

Lucky!

Dad Facts! Father's Day became an official American holiday in 1972.

What did the sun say when it was introduced to Earth?

"Pleased to heat you!"

What do you call a fake orchestra of monkeys?

A chimp-phony!

What does Dracula drive?

A monster truck!

How do you stop a bull from charging?

You unplug it!

What did the hockey player get after he stopped playing?

An off-ice job!

Where can you find a golfer on a Saturday night?

Clubbing!

What does a frog do when its car breaks down?

It gets toad away!

What kind of soda do trees like to drink?

Root beer!

> **Dad Facts!** The word "Dad" was created by babies with their baby talk.

Why did the hamburger always lose the race?

Because it could never ketchup!

What do you call a walking clock?

A time traveler!

What did one penny say to the other penny?

"We make perfect cents!"

What's luckier than finding a heads-up penny?

Finding a heads-up quarter!

Who did the zombie take to the prom?

His ghoul-friend.

What is a teacher's favorite nation?

Explanation!

Why did Mozart sell his chickens?

Because they kept saying, "Bach, Bach, Bach!"

What is a boxer's favorite drink?

Fruit *punch*!

What do aliens call a crazy space traveler?

An astro-*nut*!

What food is always cold outside the refrigerator?

Chili!

Who delivers presents to dogs?

Santa Paws!

How do you cut a wave in half?
With a *sea*-saw!

What kind of bed does a mermaid sleep in?
A waterbed!

Why did the man put money in his freezer?
He wanted cold, hard cash!

Why couldn't the pirate play cards?
Because he was sitting on the deck!

What kind of driver is needed to build a race car?
A screwdriver!

What's the best way to carve wood?
Whittle by whittle!

Why did the gamer break up with his girlfriend?
They weren't on the same level!

What did one plate say to the other?
"Dinner is on me!"

What do you call a mean cow?
Beef jerky!

What is a boxer's favorite drink?
Fruit *punch!*

What do elves learn in school?

The elf-abet!

Why are mummies so selfish?

Because they're too wrapped up in themselves!

What did the snowman say to the other snowman?

"Do you smell carrots?"

Why did the man wear a helmet when he worked on his computer?

He thought it would crash!

What is a matador's favorite sandwich?

Bull-oney!

What do you put in a barrel to make it lighter?

A hole!

How much do dead batteries charge?

Nothing. They're free of charge!

Why was the boxer fired from his job?

He never punched out!

Why do impatient people hate going to the gym?

Because of all the weights!

What should you never say to a vampire when you are mad?

"Bite me!"

What do you call an eagle who plays piano?

Talon-ted!

What did the jockey say when he fell off his horse?

"I've fallen and I can't giddy-up!"

What do you call a belt with a watch on it?

A *waist* of time!

What happens when an owl gets a sore throat?

It doesn't give a hoot!

Why was the orange so lonely?
Because the banana split!

How do you fix a jack-o'-lantern?
Give it a pumpkin patch!

What do you call a flower that runs on electricity?
A power plant!

What is a pirate's favorite kind of fish?
Goldfish!

Why was the robot angry?
Everyone kept pushing its buttons!

Why did the boy take a ruler to bed?
To see how long he slept!

What kind of lights did Noah use on the ark?
Floodlights!

Why did the jockey name his horse "Bad News"?
Because bad news travels fast!

What do you call a dentist who cleans a lion's teeth?
Brave!

What kind of horses only go out at night?
Nightmares!

How do you make a hot dog stand?
Take away its chair!

> **Dad Facts!** There are about 2 billion dads worldwide.

Why did a pie visit the dentist?
To get a new filling!

What do sprinters eat before a race?
Nothing. They fast!

Why did the lettuce win the race?
Because it was always a head!

Who is the highest-ranking officer in a cornfield?
The kernel!

When do you stop at green and go at red?
When you're eating a watermelon!

What did the sink say to the dirty dishes?
"You're in hot water now!"

What did the farmer give his family for Valentine's Day?
Hogs and kisses!

What do ghosts say when they meet?
"How do you boo?"

What's the strongest tool in the ocean?
A hammer-head shark!

Why didn't the flower ride its bike to school?
Because its petals were broken!

What kind of nails do carpenters hate hammering?
Fingernails!

What is a pirate's favorite letter in the alphabet?
Arrrr!

Why was there thunder and lightning at the elementary school?

It was time for brainstorming!

Did you hear about the angry gymnast?

She just flipped!

What do you call a lawyer who knows martial arts?

A self-defense attorney!

What is a ghost's favorite tree?

Bam-boo!

How do you find an archer?

Follow the arrows!

Why was the balloon afraid of school?

There might be a pop quiz!

What did one blade of grass say to the other during a drought?

"I guess we'll have to make dew!"

Why do French people like to eat snails?

They can't stand fast food!

What did the stamp say to the envelope on Valentine's Day?

"I'm stuck on you!"

What is it called when a snowman has a temper tantrum?

A meltdown!

Why should you be nice to a dentist?

You can hurt their fillings!

Why was the cat sitting by the computer?
To keep an eye on the mouse!

What is an astronaut's favorite part of a computer?
The space bar!

Why are police officers great volleyball players?
They're trained to serve and protect!

Why do mummies like presents?
They love the wrapping!

Dad Facts! The average age of first-time dads in the United States is 29 years old.

What did the baseball glove say to the ball?
"Catch you later!"

How do librarians catch fish?
With bookworms!

18

What's the difference between the Christmas alphabet and the regular alphabet?

The Christmas alphabet has noel!

What has four tires and flies?

A garbage truck!

What did the baby corn say to the mama corn?

"Where's pop corn?"

What asks but never answers?

An owl! (Whooo? Whooo?)

What do you call cheese that is sad?

Blue cheese!

How much did Santa pay for his sleigh?

Nothing. It was on the house!

What are two things you never eat for lunch?

Breakfast and dinner!

Which country's capital has the fastest-growing population?

Ireland. Every day it's Dublin!

What did the astronaut say to the star?

"Stop spacing out!"

Why was the student's report card wet?

It was below "C" level!

Did you hear about the math student who's afraid of negative numbers?

He'll stop at nothing to avoid them!

Why did the bowling ball keep getting into trouble?

It had a bad roll model!

Why did the bowler play another game?

He had time to spare!

What do you call skeletons who won't go to work?

Lazy bones!

Why did the golfer wear two pairs of pants?
In case he got a hole in one!

Why is a soccer stadium always cool?

It is full of fans!

Why did the teacher stop her lessons on origami?

Too much paperwork!

How did Ben Franklin feel after he discovered electricity?

He was shocked!

What do you call a greedy elf?

Elfish!

What do you call someone who pretends to be Swedish?

An artificial Swedener!

What's the difference between a dog and a marine biologist?

One wags a tail and the other tags a whale!

What does a grape say when it gets stepped on?

Nothing. It just lets out a little wine!

What do you call bears without ears?

B!

What did the astronaut cook in his skillet?

Unidentified frying objects!

What does a piece of toast wear to bed?

Jammies!

What is a cow's favorite holiday?

Moo Year's Day!

What do police officers say to their stomachs?

"You're under a vest!"

Want to hear a joke about paper?

Never mind. It's tear-able!

What kind of stories do basketball players tell?
Tall tales!

What is a vampire's favorite fruit?
A neck-tarine!

What do you call a bear with no socks on?
Bear-foot!

What is the best exercise for a swimmer?
Pool-ups!

Did you hear the joke about the sheep?
It's baaaad!

Why couldn't the lifeguard save the hippie?
The hippie was too far out, man!

How does a train eat?
It goes chew-chew!

How many apples grow on trees?
All of them!

What did the tree say to its branches when summer turned to fall?
"Leaf me alone!"

Why do tigers have stripes?
So they aren't spotted!

Who is the coolest doctor at the hospital?
The hip doctor!

Why did the computer arrive late for work?
It had a hard drive!

Why did the police officers go to the baseball game?
They heard someone was stealing bases!

Why didn't the invisible man buy a house?
He couldn't see himself living there!

Why did the baseball coach go into the kitchen?
To get a pitcher!

What do you call a snowman with a six-pack?
The Abdominal Snowman!

What did the digital clock say to its mom?
"Look Ma, no hands!"

Why did the couple buy stale bread on their wedding day?
They wanted to grow mold together!

What did the left eye say to the right eye?
"Between you and me, something smells!"

Did you hear about the dad who burned the Hawaiian pizza?
He should have put the oven on aloha temperature!

Why are pigs bad drivers?
Because they hog the road!

23

What is a duck's favorite snack?
Cheese and quackers!

What is the quietest sport?
Bowling. You can hear a pin drop!

Why are Christmas trees bad at sewing?
They keep dropping their needles!

How did the octopus beat the shark in a fight?
It was well-armed!

Did you see the snowman at the grocery store looking at carrots?
He was picking his nose!

Where did the general keep his armies?
In his sleevies!

> **Dad Facts!** Research shows that children who have close relationships with their dads are more likely to have strong social skills and more confidence.

How do trees access the internet?
They log in!

How do chickens encourage their baseball team?
They egg them on!

How often should you tell jokes about the elements?
Periodically!

What do you call two buddies who wear jackets with no sleeves?
Vest friends!

What falls in winter but never gets hurt?
Snow!

Can a kangaroo jump higher than the Statue of Liberty?
Of course! The Statue of Liberty can't jump at all!

What does a pepper do when it's angry?
It gets jalapeño face!

What should you never eat on Independence Day?
Firecrackers!

How do you weigh a fish?
Use their scales!

Do you want to hear a pizza joke?
Never mind. It's too cheesy!

Why are pirates great at shopping?
They always find the best sails!

Did you hear about the two thieves who stole a calendar?
They each got six months!

Want to hear a joke about construction?
Never mind. I'm still working on it!

How do you get a runner to remember you?
Jog their memory!

What do you call witches who live together?
Broom-mates!

How do you stop a skunk from smelling?
Hold its nose!

What do you call a crab that replaces a batter?
A pinch hitter!

Why are there no knock, knock jokes about democracy?
Because freedom rings!

Why is the scarecrow's confidence so high?
He's always outstanding in his field!

What do you call a grumpy reindeer?
Rude-olph!

Why did the grape buy guitars for its friends?
It wanted to jam!

What did the time traveler do when she was still hungry after her meal?
She went back four seconds!

What did the elephant say when it walked into the post office?
"Ouch!"

What are the strongest days of the week?
Saturday and Sunday. Every other day is a weak day!

What was Beethoven's favorite fruit?

Ba-na-na-naaaa.
Ba-na-na-naaaa!

Did you hear about the headphones that became friends?

They were earbuds!

> **Dad Facts!** According to the U.S. Census Bureau, the most common Father's Day gift is a necktie. According to fathers, it's hard to look excited when you unwrap another necktie.

Why don't basketball players go on vacation?

They aren't allowed to travel!

What do birds say on Halloween?

"Trick or tweet!"

What does a basketball genie give you?

Three swishes!

What did the dog say when he sat on sandpaper?

"Ruff!"

Why did the coach want a judge on her volleyball team?

To bring order to the court!

What did the mama spider say to her teen?

"You spend too much time on the web!"

How can you make a waterbed bouncier?

Use spring water!

Did you hear about the celebrity who accidentally glued himself to his autobiography?

That's his story and he's sticking to it!

What animal has more lives than a cat?

Frogs. They croak every night!

How do you throw a party in space?
You planet!

Why did the policeman give the sheep a ticket?
She made an illegal ewe turn!

Where can you get a haircut and a hot dog?
A barber-Q!

What did the big flower say to the little flower?
"Hi, bud!"

What do you call a pig that wins the lottery?
Filthy rich!

Did you hear about the optometrist who loved jokes?
The cornea the better!

What word starts with "E," ends with "E," and has only one letter in it?
Envelope!

What is it called when a basketball player misses a dunk?
Alley-oops!

Why do hockey rinks have curved corners?
If they were 90 degrees, the ice would melt!

What do you call a horse that lives next door?
A neigh-bor!

What do you call it when a cat wins at the dog show?
A cat-has-trophy!

What do you call a deer that costs a dollar?
A buck!

Why are cheetahs terrible at hide-and-seek?
They're always spotted!

Why don't snails fart?
Their houses don't have windows!

What do you call a dirty hippo?
A hippopota-mess!

Why are giraffes slow to apologize?
It takes them an extra-long time to swallow their pride!

Where do dogs park?
In a barking lot!

Why did the teddy bear say no to dessert?
Because it was stuffed!

Why do fish live in salt water?
Because pepper makes them sneeze!

What kind of dog chases anything that's red?
A bulldog!

Why did the cat run away from the tree?
It was scared of the bark!

Why do rabbits love carrots?
No bunny knows!

Why do porcupines always win their games?
They start with the most points!

Why can't you hear it when a pterodactyl goes to the bathroom?
Because the "p" is silent!

What do you call a sleeping bull?
A bulldozer!

Why can't you play basketball with pigs?

They always hog the ball!

What do you call a pony with a sore throat?

A little horse!

What do you call a pile of kittens?

A meowtain!

What do you call an elephant that doesn't matter?

An irrelephant!

Why don't ants get sick?

They have all the right antibodies!

What type of markets do dogs avoid?

Flea markets!

What is a cat's favorite color?

Purrr-ple!

Why do ducks have feathers?

To cover their butt quacks!

Why do bears have hairy coats?

Fur protection!

How do skeletons call each other?

With tele-bones!

Would you like to hear a joke about dogs?

Never mind. It's a little far-fetched!

What is the best advice you can give a baseball player?

If you don't succeed at first, try second base!

Why does a pitcher raise one leg when he pitches?

If he raises both legs, he will fall down!

What do you call a dinosaur with an extensive vocabulary?

A thesaurus!

Why couldn't the keyboard get a hat out of its closet?

The CAPS LOCK was on!

What do you call a nose with no body?

Nobody nose!

What do a dog and phone have in common?

They both have collar ID!

Where do sheep go on vacation?

The Baaaaahamas!

What's more amazing than a talking llama?

A spelling bee!

Why does Humpty Dumpty love autumn?

Because he always has a great fall!

Did you hear about the almond who ate vegetables, ran every morning, and took vitamins?

It was a total health nut!

What do you call a bear with no teeth?

A gummy bear!

Did you know the first French fries weren't actually cooked in France?

They were cooked in Greece!

Where does a snowman keep his money?

In a snowbank!

What did one hat say to the other?
"You stay here. I'll go on ahead!"

Why are skunks so emotional?
They are very scent-imental!

How does the moon cut his hair?
Eclipse it!

What time do ducks wake up?
At the quack of dawn!

> **Dad Facts!** More than 2.25 billion cups of coffee are consumed in the world every day.

What kind of birds work at construction sites?
Cranes!

Why is it hard to steal third base?
There's a short stop on the way!

Why don't baseball players lock their doors?
They are always safe at home!

Why did the cookie go to the doctor?
Because he felt crummy!

What kind of street does a ghost live on?
A dead end!

What do you call two banana peels?
Slippers!

Why is a room full of married people still considered empty?

There isn't a single person in it!

What is the best season to jump on a trampoline?

Spring time!

Where do you learn to make ice cream?

Sundae school!

What do you call an alligator wearing a vest?

An investi-gator!

Why wouldn't the crab share its treasure?

It was a little shellfish!

Why do seagulls fly over the sea?

If they flew over the bay, they would be bay-gulls!

Why is dark spelled with a "k" and not a "c"?

Because you can't "c" in the dark!

How much money does a pirate pay for corn?

A buccaneer!

Who is in charge of school supplies?

The ruler!

Why do dogs love baseball?

They always get walked!

What kind of dogs do vampires like?

Bloodhounds!

Why don't koalas count as bears?

They don't have the koala-fications!

Why do bees have sticky hair?

Because they use a honeycomb!

33

**What kind of haircuts
do bees get?**

Buzzzz cuts!

**What's worse than finding
a worm in your apple?**

Finding half of a worm!

**Have you seen the
new candy canes?**

They're in mint condition!

**Did you hear about the
restaurant on the moon?**

Great food. No atmosphere!

**What is the best day
to go to the beach?**

Sunday!

**What kind of room can
you never enter?**

A mushroom!

**What did one crooked
tooth say to the other?**

"Brace yourself!"

**Why did the old man
fall down the well?**

He couldn't see that well!

**What's more useful
than the invention of
the first telephone?**

The second one!

**Why are robots
never afraid?**

Because they have
nerves of steel!

**Who has the smelliest
position in football?**

The scenter!

**What is a ghost's
favorite dessert?**

I scream!

**What would a vampire
never order to eat?**

A stake!

**How do you know
when a squirrel has
eaten too much?**

It acts like a nut!

34

Where do young cows eat lunch?
In the calf-eteria!

What do you call cheese that isn't yours?
Nacho cheese!

Why did the girl throw a stick of butter?
She wanted to see a butterfly!

What country do sharks come from?
Finland!

What time do you go to the dentist?
Tooth-hurty!

How do you stop an astronaut's baby from crying?
You rocket!

Why did the girl bring a ladder to school?
She wanted to go to high school!

What do you call a fake noodle?
An impasta!

Where do pencils come from?
Pencil-vania!

Why did the football coach put a ninja in the game?
To run a sneak play!

Why do soccer players do well in school?
They know how to use their heads!

What room are ghosts never allowed to use?
A living room!

35

What do lawyers wear to court?
Lawsuits!

What has ears but cannot see?

A cornfield!

What did the picture say to the wall?

"Help! I've been framed!"

Why did the student eat her homework?

The teacher said it was a piece of cake!

Dad Facts! Wisdom teeth are called wisdom teeth because they are the last teeth to grow, when people are older and wiser.

What did Neptune say to Saturn?

"Give me a ring sometime!"

How did the soccer goalie get rich?

She loved to save!

Why couldn't the astronaut book a hotel on the moon?

Because it was full!

Why did the teacher jump in the pool?

She wanted to test the water!

Why are shoemakers such good people?

They have good soles!

Where do baby ghosts go during the day?

To day-scare centers!

What did the book put on when it was cold?

A jacket!

What do you get when you cross an elephant and a fish?

Swimming trunks!

How did the phone propose to its girlfriend?

It gave her a ring!

How do pickles enjoy a day out?
They relish it!

What did the pickle say to the cucumber?
"I'm kind of a big dill!"

Why didn't the orange win the race?
It ran out of juice!

What did the boat say to the pier?
"What's up, dock?"

What did the painter say to his girlfriend?
"I love you with all my art!"

Why did the soccer coach put a magician in the game?
He was the best at hat tricks!

How do you know referees love their job?
They whistle while they work!

Why are ghosts bad liars?
Because you can see right through them!

Why couldn't the pirate learn the alphabet?
Because he was always lost at "c"!

What did the wolf say when it stubbed its toe?
"Howwwwwwwl!"

What kind of music makes rabbits want to dance?

Hip hop!

Why do bananas put on suntan lotion?

Because they don't want to peel!

Why did the tomato blush?

Because it saw the salad dressing!

Where do cars go for a swim?

The carpool!

What kind of award did the dentist receive?

A little plaque!

How do hairstylists get to work so fast?

They take shortcuts!

What is a bird's favorite type of math?

Owl-gebra!

Why is six afraid of seven?

Because seven *ate* nine!

Why didn't the hockey player have a good game?

He got cold feet!

What do hockey players drink on hot days?

Iced tea!

What instrument do skeletons play best?

The trom-bone!

What kind of key can't open doors?

A monkey!

Dad Facts! The Air Guitar World Championships take place every year in Finland, where the event started in 1996.

What did the hamburger give his sweetheart?

An onion ring!

What fruit do scarecrows love the most?

Straw-berries!

What did the pirate say on his 80th birthday?

"Aye matey!"

What kind of haircuts do pirates get?

Crew cuts!

What do you call a sheep covered in chocolate?

A candy baaaaaaa!

What is a pirate's favorite exercise?

The plank!

Why shouldn't you argue with a decimal?

Because decimals always have a point!

Where do elephants pack their clothes?

In their trunks!

How do you make an egg giggle?

Tell it a funny yolk!

Why should you not talk to pi?

Because it will go on forever!

You know what's odd?

Every other number!

What did one light bulb say to the other light bulb?

"I love you watts and watts!"

Why shouldn't you tell a secret on a farm?

Because the potatoes have eyes and corn has ears!

What is a golfer's worst nightmare?

The bogey-man!

Why did the golfer keep an umbrella nearby?

In case of a bad "fore" cast!

Dad Facts! Dads have enjoyed pancakes for thousands of years. The earliest pancakes were made by ancient Greeks and Romans. These early pancakes were often sweetened with honey.

Why was the tennis court so loud?

All of the players raised a racket!

What did one toilet say to the other?

"You look a bit flushed!"

What do you call a cheeseburger in a race car?

Fast food!

How do snowboarders get to school?

By icicle!

What did the Dalmatian say after lunch?

"That hit the spot!"

Why couldn't the twins play volleyball?

They already had a match!

Why shouldn't you fall in love with a tennis player?

To them, "love" means nothing!

What do you call a witch who loves the beach?

A sand-witch!

What do you call a slow snow skier?

A slope-poke!

41

Knock Yourself Out

Who's There? Knock, Knock Jokes!

When knock, knock jokes were invented in the 1930s, they were cool—like, really cool—or swell, as they said at the time. They were on radio shows and in newspapers. Musicians told knock, knock jokes in the middle of their songs, and large crowds showed up for knock, knock contests. They were a cultural phenomenon, and nearly 100 years after the peak of their popularity, we're still telling them. That's impressive. But it shouldn't be surprising.

Knock, knock jokes are perfect for kids. They have a formula that's easy to understand and repeat. Each joke is like a short story with suspense and a silly surprise. When somebody says, "Knock, knock," you want to answer. So, what are you waiting for? Knock yourself out with the punch lines in these knock, knock jokes!

Knock, knock.
Who's there?
Lettuce.
Lettuce who?
**Lettuce in, it's cold out
here!**

Knock, knock.
Who's there?
Alaska.
Alaska who?
**Alaska to open the door
one last time!**

Knock, knock.
Who's there?
Garden.
Garden who?
**Garden the treasure. We
have to protect it!**

Knock, knock.
Who's there?
Justin.
Justin who?
Justin time for dinner!

Knock, knock.
Who's there?
Wooden shoe.
Wooden shoe who?
**Wooden shoe like to hear
another joke?**

Knock, knock.
Who's there?
Pig.
Pig who?
**Pig up your clothes.
Your room is a mess!**

Knock, knock.
Who's there?
Grammar.
Grammar who?
Grammar and Grandpa!

Knock, knock.
Who's there?
Spell.
Spell who?
W-H-O!

Knock, knock.
Who's there?
Hawaii.
Hawaii who?
I'm fine, Hawaii you?

Knock, knock.
Who's there?
Water.
Water who?
**Water you doing
right now?**

Knock, knock.
Who's there?
Minnow.
Minnow who?
Let minnow what you think!

Knock, knock.
Who's there?
Phillip.
Phillip who?
Phillip my plate with chicken nuggets!

Knock, knock.
Who's there?
Pecan.
Pecan who?
Pecan somebody your own size!

Knock, knock.
Who's there?
Wilma.
Wilma who?
Wilma dinner be ready soon? It smells delicious!

Knock, knock.
Who's there?
Alpaca.
Alpaca who?
Alpaca suitcase. Let's go on a trip!

Knock, knock.
Who's there?
Goat.
Goat who?
**Goat to the door to see
who's knocking!**

Dad Facts! Babies need 2,500 to 3,000 diapers in their first year and an average of 6,000 to 8,000 diapers by the time they are potty trained.

Knock, knock.
Who's there?
Weed.
Weed who?
Weed need to open the door to find out!

Knock, knock.
Who's there?
Division.
Division who?
Division test is hard if you close your eyes!

Knock, knock.
Who's there?
Diana.
Diana who?
Diana thirst. Can I please have some water?!

Knock, knock.
Who's there?
Bully.
Bully who?
Bully-ve me, it's better to be nice!

Knock, knock.
Who's there?
Claire.
Claire who?
Claire the doorway, I'm coming in!

Knock, knock.
Who's there?
Safari.
Safari who?
Sa-fari, so good!

Knock, knock.
Who's there?
Soup.
Soup who?
Soup-er man!

Knock, knock.
Who's there?
Gopher.
Gopher who?
Gopher it. You can do it!

47

Knock, knock.
Who's there?
Jello.
Jello who?
Jello, is anybody home?

Knock, knock.
Who's there?
Howie.
Howie who?
Howie gonna get in the house if you don't open the door?

Knock, knock.
Who's there?
Jess.
Jess who?
Jess open the door!

Knock, knock.
Who's there?
Ice.
Ice who?
Ice said it was me!

Knock, knock.
Who's there?
Europe.
Europe who?
Europe-ning the door!

Knock, knock.
Who's there?
Warrior.
Warrior who?
Warrior been? We've been waiting on you!

Knock, knock.
Who's there?
Repeat.
Repeat who?
Who, who, who, who...

Knock, knock.
Who's there?
Chick.
Chick who?
Chick your shoelaces, they're untied!

Knock, knock.
Who's there?
Stopwatch.
Stopwatch who?
Stopwatch you're doing right now!

Knock, knock.
Who's there?
Butterfly.
Butterfly who?
Butterfly if you visit Australia.

Knock, knock.
Who's there?
Armageddon.
Armageddon who?
Armageddon tired of doing all of this knocking!

Knock, knock.
Who's there?
France.
France who?
France-y seeing you here!

Knock, knock.
Who's there?
Hurricane.
Hurricane who?
Hurricane you bring me an umbrella?

Knock, knock.
Who's there?
Wyatt.
Wyatt who?
Wyatt taking so long to answer the door?

Knock, knock.
Who's there?
Goldfish.
Goldfish who?
**Enough with the questions.
Put me back in the bowl!**

Knock, knock.
Who's there?
Anita.
Anita who?
Anita go to the bathroom, let me in!

Knock, knock.
Who's there?
Cook.
Cook who?
Did you call me "cuckoo"? How rude!

> **Dad Facts!** Steaks are graded based on quality and consistency. In the United States, the USDA grades are Prime, Choice, and Select, with Prime being the highest quality.

Knock, knock.
Who's there?
Donut.
Donut who?
Donut leave without locking the door!

Knock, knock.
Who's there?
Stu.
Stu who?
Stu late. Time for bed!

Knock, knock.
Who's there?
Will.
Will who?
Will you let me in?

Knock, knock.
Who's there?
Leaf.
Leaf who?
Leaf what you're doing and come here!

Knock, knock.
Who's there?
Utah.
Utah who?
Utah-king to me?

Knock, knock.
Who's there?
Radio.
Radio who?
Radio not, here I come!

51

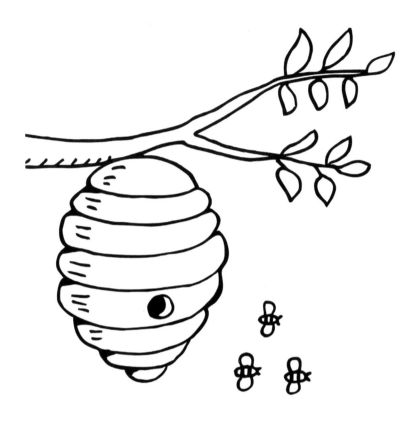

Knock, knock.
Who's there?
Beehive.
Beehive who?
Beehive yourself or you'll get into trouble!

Knock, knock.
Who's there?
May.
May who?
May I please come in?

Knock, knock.
Who's there?
Cows go.
Cows go who?
No, cows go "Moo!"

Knock, knock.
Who's there?
Cargo.
Cargo who?
Cargo *vroom vroom!*

Knock, knock.
Who's there?
Fairy.
Fairy who?
Fairy nice of you to open the door!

Knock, knock.
Who's there?
Norway.
Norway who?
Norway I'm leaving before you open this door!

Knock, knock.
Who's there?
Hayden.
Hayden who?
Hayden seek is my favorite game!

Knock, knock.
Who's there?
Noah.
Noah who?
Noah good place to eat?

Knock, knock.
Who's there?
Omelet.
Omelet who?
Omelet you know once you open the door!

Knock, knock.
Who's there?
Robin.
Robin who?
Robin you! Give me your money!

Knock, knock.
Who's there?
Peeka.
Peeka who?
Peeka-boo!

53

Knock, knock.
Who's there?
Scold.
Scold who?
S'cold out here. I want to come inside!

Knock, knock.
Who's there?
Mind.
Mind who?
Mind your manners and say, "hello!"

Knock, knock.
Who's there?
Venice.
Venice who?
Venice the party starting?

Knock, knock.
Who's there?
Pasture.
Pasture who?
Pasture bedtime, isn't it?

Knock, knock.
Who's there?
Wendy.
Wendy who?
Wendy doorbell gonna get fixed?

Knock, knock.
Who's there?
Amanda.
Amanda who?
Amanda fix your doorbell!

Knock, knock.
Who's there?
Bread.
Bread who?
Bread any good books lately?

Dad Facts! The heaviest land animal is the African elephant, which can weigh up to 15,000 pounds. The heaviest overall animal is the blue whale, which weighs up to 330,000 pounds.

Knock, knock.
Who's there?
Luke.
Luke who?
Luke out the window and you'll see!

Knock, knock.
Who's there?
Lena.
Lena who?
Lena little closer, and I'll tell you a joke!

Knock, knock.
Who's there?
Paul.
Paul who?
Paul up a chair and I'll tell you!

Knock, knock.
Who's there?
Honeydew.
Honeydew who?
Honeydew you want to go to the movies tonight?

Knock, knock.
Who's there?
Thunder.
Thunder who?
Thunder the bed!

Knock, knock.
Who's there?
Jamaica.
Jamaica who?
Jamaica dinner yet? I'm hungry!

Knock, knock.
Who's there?
Doorway.
Doorway who?
Door weigh too much, help me open it!

Knock, knock.
Who's there?
Needle.
Needle who?
Needle lil' help with this doorknob!

Knock, knock.
Who's there?
Some bunny.
Some bunny who?
Some bunny who is tired of all these questions!

Knock, knock.
Who's there?
Spin.
Spin who?
Spin a while since I've been here. Good to see you!

55

Knock, knock.
Who's there?
Gorilla.
Gorilla who?
Gorilla hamburger for me, please!

Knock, knock.
Who's there?
Red.
Red who?
Ready or not, I'm coming in!

Knock, knock.
Who's there?
House.
House who?
House you gonna know if you don't answer the door!

Knock, knock.
Who's there?
Tokyo.
Tokyo who?
Tokyo long enough to answer the door!

Knock, knock.
Who's there?
Island.
Island who?
Island at noon. Can you pick me up?

Knock, knock.
Who's there?
Goliath.
Goliath who?
Go-liath down, thou look-eth sleepy!

Knock, knock.
Who's there?
Freddie.
Freddie who?
Freddie or not, here I come!

Knock, knock.
Who's there?
Linda.
Linda who?
Linda hand, I can't do this all by myself!

Knock, knock.
Who's there?
Arthur.
Arthur who?
Arthur any cookies inside? I'm hungry!

Knock, knock.
Who's there?
Goose.
Goose who?
Goose who it is!

Knock, knock.
Who's there?
Rufus.
Rufus who?
Rufus leaking and I'm getting wet!

Knock, knock.
Who's there?
Mikey.
Mikey who?
Mikey isn't working and the door is locked!

Knock, knock.
Who's there?
Butter.
Butter who?
It's butter if you don't know!

Knock, knock.
Who's there?
Yukon.
Yukon who?
Yukon say that again!

Knock, knock.
Who's there?
High tide.
High tide who?
High tide calling, but nobody answered.

Knock, knock.
Who's there?
Tex.
Tex who?
Tex me a message and I'll tell you!

Knock, knock.
Who's there?
Tell.
Tell who?
Tell ya later!

Knock, knock.
Who's there?
Mustache.
Mustache who?
Mustache you a question, but I'll shave it for later!

Knock, knock.
Who's there?
Baby owl.
Baby owl who?
**Baby owl see you later.
Maybe I won't.**

> **Dad Facts!** The moon is nearly 240,000 miles away from Earth. It takes astronauts three days to get there.

Knock, knock.
Who's there?
Irish.
Irish who?
**Irish you a Happy
St. Patrick's Day!**

Knock, knock.
Who's there?
Annie.
Annie who?
Annie-body home?

Knock, knock.
Who's there?
Yo.
Yo who?
Not yo *who*, yo *ho*—I'm a pirate!

Knock, knock.
Who's there?
Common.
Common who?
Common get it!

Knock, knock.
Who's there?
Broom.
Broom who?
Broom, broom, it's a motorcycle.

59

Knock, knock.
Who's there?
Yam.
Yam who?
I yam who I am!

Knock, knock.
Who's there?
Ladybug.
Ladybug who?
Ladybug someone else for a while.

Knock, knock.
Who's there?
Pete.
Pete who?
Pete-za delivery!

Knock, knock.
Who's there?
Abe.
Abe who?
Abe-e, C, D, E, F, G...

Knock, knock.
Who's there?
Felix.
Felix who?
Felix-hausted. Let me in!

Knock, knock.
Who's there?
Alex.
Alex who?
Alex-splain later!

Knock, knock.
Who's there?
Peas.
Peas who?
Peas be nice and let me inside!

Knock, knock.
Who's there?
Says.
Says who?
Says me. That's who!

Dad Facts! The first person to go faster than the speed of sound was Captain Charles "Chuck" Yeager, a U.S. Air Force officer and test pilot, in 1947.

Knock, knock.
Who's there?
Howl.
Howl who?
Howl you know unless you open the door?

61

Knock, knock.
Who's there?
Closure.
Closure who?
Closure book and open the door!

Knock, knock.
Who's there?
Flower.
Flower who?
Flower you feeling?

Knock, knock.
Who's there?
Miss.
Miss who?
Miss-placed my key!

Knock, knock.
Who's there?
Nathan.
Nathan who?
Nathan to see here!

Knock, knock.
Who's there?
Sarah.
Sarah who?
Sarah problem here?

Knock, knock.
Who's there?
Ice cream soda.
Ice cream soda who?
Ice cream soda people can hear me!

Knock, knock.
Who's there?
A herd.
A herd who?
A herd you were home, so I came over!

Knock, knock.
Who's there?
Olive.
Olive who?
Olive you!

Knock, knock.
Who's there?
Harvey.
Harvey who?
Harvey gonna play some ball?

Knock, knock.
Who's there?
Hal.
Hal who?
Hal-o? Anybody home?

Knock, knock.
Who's there?
Frank.
Frank who?
Frank you for opening the door!

Knock, knock.
Who's there?
Weirdo.
Weirdo who?
Weirdo you think you're going?

Knock, knock.
Who's there?
Waterfall.
Waterfall who?
Waterfall these people doing here?

Dad Facts! International Talk Like a Pirate Day encourages people to dress and talk like pirates every year on September 19.

Knock, knock.
Who's there?
Noise.
Noise who?
Noise to see you!

Knock, knock.
Who's there?
Iguana.
Iguana who?
Iguana play. Can you come out?

Knock, knock.
Who's there?
Ears.
Ears who?
Ears another knock, knock joke for you!

Knock, knock.
Who's there?
Witch.
Witch who?
Witch way to the haunted house?

Knock, knock.
Who's there?
Anabel.
Anabel who?
Anabel go ring, ring!

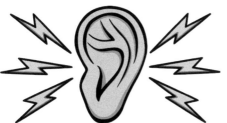

63

Knock, knock.
Who's there?
Cloudy.
Cloudy who?
Cloudy, partner! Yee-haw!

Knock, knock.
Who's there?
Jim.
Jim who?
Jim mind if I come in and
play with you?

Knock, knock.
Who's there?
Isabelle.
Isabelle who?
Isabelle not working? I had
to knock.

Knock, knock.
Who's there?
Ooze.
Ooze who?
Ooze in charge around
here?

Knock, knock.
Who's there?
Letter.
Letter who?
Letter in or she'll knock
down the door!

Knock, knock.
Who's there?
Icing.
Icing who?
Icing so loudly that
everyone can hear me!

Knock, knock.
Who's there?
Bunny
Bunny who?
Some bunny been eating
my carrots.

Knock, knock.
Who's there?
Orange.
Orange who?
Orange you glad to see me?

Knock, knock.
Who's there?
Candice.
Candice who?
Candice door open?

Knock, knock.
Who's there?
Abby.
Abby who?
Abby birthday to you!

Knock, knock.
Who's there?
A little ole lady.
A little ole lady who?
I didn't know you could yodel!

Knock, knock.
Who's there?
Thunder.
Thunder who?
Thunder wear is dirty. It needs to be washed.

Knock, knock.
Who's there?
June.
June who?
June know how long I've been knocking out here?

Knock, knock.
Who's there?
Mary.
Mary who?
Mary Christmas!

Knock, knock.
Who's there?
Beats.
Beats who?
Beats me!

Knock, knock.
Who's there?
Alex.
Alex who?
Alex the questions around here!

Knock, knock.
Who's there?
Emma.
Emma who?
Emma need you to unlock the door!

Knock, knock.
Who's there?
Sherwood.
Sherwood who?
Sherwood like a juice box. Do you have one inside?

Knock, knock.
Who's there?
Juicy.
Juicy who?
Juicy what I see?

Knock, knock.
Who's there?
Freeze.
Freeze who?
Freeze a jolly good fellow.

Knock, knock.
Who's there?
Turnip.
Turnip who?
Turnip the music. Let's dance!

Knock, knock.
Who's there?
Izzy.
Izzy who?
Izzy home? Or Izzie out?

> **Dad Facts!** The largest U.S. currency ever printed was a $100,000 bill. It featured President Woodrow Wilson.

Knock, knock.
Who's there?
Gwen.
Gwen who?
Gwen will you open the door?

Knock, knock.
Who's there?
Mayo.
Mayo who?
Mayo dreams all come true!

Knock, knock.
Who's there?
Sir.
Sir who?
Sir-prise! It's me!

Knock, knock.
Who's there?
Sadie.
Sadie who?
Sadie magic word and I'll go away!

Knock, knock.
Who's there?
Ben.
Ben who?
Ben waiting for you to admit you don't remember my last name!

Knock, knock.
Who's there?
Adore.
Adore who?
Adore is between us. Please open it!

Knock, knock.
Who's there?
Cash.
Cash who?
No thanks. Do you have any pecans?

Knock, knock.
Who's there?
Phyllis.
Phyllis who?
Phyllis in on everything that happened since we last spoke!

Knock, knock.
Who's there?
Egg.
Egg who?
Egg-cellent, you're home. Let's go play!

Knock, knock.
Who's there?
Candy.
Candy who?
Candy person who blocked my driveway please move their car?

Dad Facts! During the 1912 Olympics, Jim Thorpe became the first Native American to win a gold medal. More remarkably, he won a gold medal wearing mismatched shoes he found in the trash after his own shoes went missing.

Knock, knock.
Who's there?
Hike.
Hike who?
I didn't know you liked Japanese poetry!

Knock, knock.
Who's there?
Dewey.
Dewey who?
Dewey have to keep doing knock, knock jokes?

69

Punny Because It's True

The Pun-believable Wisdom of Dads

Puns are words with playful twists on the meaning. The most common puns are homophones, homographs, and homonyms.

Homophones are words that sound the same with different meanings and spellings such as two, to, and too. Homographs are spelled the same with different meanings, like bass guitar and bass fishing. Homonyms are spelled the same and sound the same with different meanings, like baseball bat and vampire bat.

You can also create your own puns by making up words like paw-some for something awesome involving pets or pun-believable for the wisdom of dad puns. That's why the jokes in this chapter combine the wisdom of dads with our punny sense of humor.

If a friend challenges you to a bird pun contest, remember toucan play that game.

If you are impressed by a talking parrot, you should hear a spelling bee.

When people find out you are a bad electrician, they will be shocked.

Becoming a vegetarian is a missed steak.

Palm trees don't fit as easily in your hand as they sound.

Don't get a brain transplant. You will change your mind.

Learn sign language. It's very handy.

Don't wash a car with your brother. Use a sponge instead.

Stale bread is a leading cause of crumby days.

When you see a piano falling down a mineshaft, you can hear A-flat minor.

Don't trust atoms. They make up everything.

Don't be sloppy. Act like a peacock and show attention to de tail.

If you ask for a vegetable joke, it might be corny.

A universal remote control isn't as powerful as it sounds.

If you forget how to catch a boomerang, stay alert. It will come back to you.

Dad Facts! There are more than 600,000 words in the English language. That's a lot of potential for pun jokes!

The postal service is a mail-dominated industry.

No matter how much you push the envelope, it will still be stationary.

When you talk about the sea, it sounds very deep.

If you can't hack it as a lumberjack, they will give you the axe.

Too many dad jokes can make you feel numb, but math jokes can make you feel number.

Don't make fun of polka music. It's not nice accordion to a recent study.

Don't try to make reservations at the library. It's always booked.

Origami is tough because the challenge is always in creasing.

Don't wear glasses when you play football. It's a contact sport.

Burglars are sensitive because they take things personally.

Elevators can be helpful and drive you up a wall at the same time.

When somebody takes a bad photo of you, make them give it back.

If somebody asks you to make them a sandwich, don't squeeze them between two slices of bread.

Ranch dressing is just a fancy name for cowboy clothes.

The rotation of the Earth will make your day.

Tip your waiters. They bring a lot to the table.

You can be outstanding simply by standing outside.

The things that make you smile are your facial muscles.

Don't eat clocks. It's too time-consuming.

Don't trust people who say age is just a number. It's just a word.

Sundays might be a little sad, but the day before is a Saturday.

There are three types of people: Those who can count and those who can't.

Before you tell jokes about retired people, remember that none of them work.

If you're afraid of elevators, there are steps you can take to avoid them.

Don't ask skunks for money.
They'll only give you one scent.

You can't be a doctor if you don't have patients.

Don't spell "part" backward. It's a trap.

> **Dad Facts!** President George Washington didn't know dinosaurs existed. The word "dinosaur" was established in 1841, more than 100 years after Washington was born. Before then, dinosaurs were associated with dragons and other mythological creatures.

When you are color-blind, the diagnosis can come completely out of the purple.

If at first you don't succeed, skydiving is not for you.

When a woman gives birth, she's just kidding.

If somebody only knows 25 letters of the alphabet, ask them if they know Y.

Don't trust stairs. They are always up to something.

You can hate facial hair, but don't be surprised if it grows on you.

Don't believe people who say they picked their nose. They were born with their nose just like the rest of us.

Tell dad jokes. He will think you're funny.

Don't let your mind wander unless you know it will come back.

Time flies like an arrow. Fruit flies like a banana.

Before you fight fire with fire, remember that fire marshals suggest water.

When you have a bladder infection, urine trouble. See a doctor.

Cats are friendliest when they're feline fine.

If you're worried about a speed bump, try to get over it slowly.

I'm always sick on school days because I have a weekend immune system.

Don't put wallpaper on yourself. It looks better on the wall.

The most musical pet you can get is a trumpet.

No matter what you think about people from Switzerland, their flag is a big plus.

If all of your socks have holes in them, don't throw them out. That's where you put your feet inside them.

The largest pickle is a really big dill.

Don't be a banker if there's a chance you will lose interest.

Velcro? It's a rip-off!

A golf ball is a golf ball no matter how you putt it.

You can lead a horse to water, but a pencil must be lead.

Every theatrical performance is a play on words.

The fastest way to get fired at a calendar factory is to take a day off.

A fly without wings is a walk.

Giraffes can grow up to 18 feet, but they usually only have four.

80

Getting paid to sleep is a dream job.

Reading while sunbathing makes you well red.

Cannibals like to meat people, but not in a friendly way.

Parmesan cheese is grate for you.

If you stay up late to see where the sun goes at night, it will eventually dawn on you.

> **Dad Facts!** Bowling is a sport that has been played since 3200 BCE in ancient Egypt.

Inspecting mirrors is a job you can see yourself doing.

If you don't want dry skin, don't use a towel.

Frogs are happy because they eat whatever bugs them.

The best service animal for tardiness is a watchdog.

If your dog feels warm and needs medicine, ketchup is best for a hot dog.

If you can't find where to milk a cow, try the udder side.

You can tell carrots are good for your eyesight by what you don't see— rabbits wearing glasses.

If you want to try a sport just for kicks, soccer is the logical choice.

The best way to get wavy hair is to dip it in the ocean.

Hills are so much easier to climb than mountains, it's hill-arious.

Dad Facts! November 6 is National Nacho Day. Celebrate with nachos and cheese-y jokes!

Throw them out when you need them. Take them back when you don't need them. That's boat anchors for ya.

If you want to give a friend a groundbreaking gift, give them a shovel.

Too many birthdays are bad for your health.

If you enjoy seeing stunning things, you'll love a taser.

If you don't want to get mugged, stay out of coffee shops.

Can February march? No, but April may.

Wearing glasses while doing math improves division.

If Ford invented the airplane,
it wouldn't have been Wright.

Trees are shady.

Statisticians love math and then sum, but it isn't necessary.

You can tell bread is lazy because it's always loafing around.

Books about antigravity are hard to put down.

If you can't play piano by ear, use your hands.

When you're down and need an uplifting experience, use the elevator.

Melons have weddings because they cantaloupe.

The strongest sea creatures are mussels!

A great factory will always be better than a satisfactory.

**The circus isn't relaxing.
It's in tents.**

If you want to make some real dough, work at a bakery.

The tallest building doesn't have the most stories. A library does.

Scientists with bad breath should try more experi-mints.

Whenever a teacher erases a whiteboard, it's re-markable.

Friends addicted to the Hokey Pokey will eventually turn themselves around.

Don't trust people who do acupuncture. They're backstabbers.

Don't bet against a chiropractor who says they can fix your posture. You will stand corrected.

When a math teacher calls you average, it's mean.

Singers who can't find the right key will be locked out of their house until they do.

Parallel lines have so much in common. It's a shame they'll never meet.

The heaviest food you can order is won-ton soup.

If you want a job in the lotion industry, apply daily.

Graveyards must be crowded because people are dying to get in.

You should appreciate your water before you boil it, because it will be mist.

Don't hire people named William if you don't like paying bills.

If you want a stable business, buy a horse farm.

No matter how you say it, drool rolls off the tongue.

A house without numbers is something that needs to be addressed.

When someone tells you to jump in a hole full of water, they mean well.

When a clock shows **6:30**, it is the best time, hands down.

Murphy's Law says anything that can go wrong, will go wrong. Cole's Law is shredded cabbage mixed with mayonnaise.

The last thing you need is a burial plot.

A Riddle Bit More

Riddles for Giggles

Dads want to be funny. But we also want you to know we're smart. So how do dads do both? Funny riddles.

Riddles and jokes both use clever wordplay, encourage creative thinking, and finish with a fun twist. When riddles are funny, they *are* jokes. This is the sweet spot for dads trying to entertain kids in a thought-provoking way.

Whether you're right or wrong, a riddle challenges your mind, encourages deep thinking, and sparks curiosity. And when a dad is asking the riddle, he sounds smart—and he is smart because he's promoting critical thinking. If he's funny, too, he won't stop you from calling him a genius.

You don't need to be a genius to solve the riddles in this chapter. All you need is a sense of curiosity and a sense of humor.

What has four legs but can't walk?
A table.

What has many rings but no fingers?
A telephone.

What has a neck but no head?
A bottle.

> **Dad Facts!** The world's fastest animal is the peregrine falcon. It can fly more than 240 miles per hour when pursuing prey.

What is so fragile that saying its name breaks it?
Silence.

What goes up but never comes back down?
Your age.

What has four i's but can't see?
Mississippi.

What is orange and sounds like a parrot?
A carrot.

What is easy to get into but hard to get out of?
Trouble.

What belongs to you but is used more by others?
Your name.

What asks no questions but requires many answers?

A doorbell.

You can keep it only after giving it to someone. What is it?

Your word.

What is round on both sides but high in the middle?

Ohio.

What goes up and down but never moves?

A flight of stairs.

What goes in and around the house but never touches it?

The sun.

What match can you never put in a matchbox?

A tennis match.

What runs all day but never gets anywhere?

A refrigerator.

How far can a fox run into the woods?
Only halfway. Otherwise, it would be running out of the woods.

I babble but I can't talk. What am I?

A brook.

What question can you never answer "yes" to?

"Are you asleep?"

Eric throws a ball as hard as he can. It comes back to him, even though nothing and nobody has touched it. How?

He throws it straight up in the air.

What has hands but doesn't clap?

A clock.

What is shaped like a box, has no feet, and runs up and down?

An elevator.

While looking at a photograph, a man said, "Brothers and sisters have I none. That man's father is my father's son." Who was the person in the photograph?

The man's son.

What comes once in a minute, twice in a moment, but never in a thousand years?

The letter "m."

With what two animals do most people go to bed?

Two calves.

What goes up and down but never moves?

The temperature.

The more I appear, the less you see. What is it I could be?

Darkness.

What is the difference between the North Pole and the South Pole?
The world.

What is the last thing you take off before you get in bed?
Your feet off the floor.

What invention allows you to look right through a wall?
A window.

You throw away the outside and cook the inside, then you eat the outside and throw away the inside. What is it?
Corn on the cob. You throw away the husk, cook and eat the kernels, then you throw away the cob.

Name three consecutive days when none of the seven days of the week appear.
Yesterday, today, and tomorrow.

I am always in front of you, but you will never see me. What am I?
The future.

A doctor and a boy were fishing. The boy was the doctor's son, but the doctor was not the boy's father. Who was the doctor?
His mother.

What has teeth but doesn't use them for eating?
A comb.

How do you make the number one disappear?
Add the letter "g" and it's "gone."

What bank never has any money?
A riverbank.

What is bought by the yard and worn by the foot?
Carpet.

I make a loud noise when I am changing. I get lighter as I get bigger. What am I?
Popcorn.

I can be any color you can imagine. You see me in everyday life. I've existed for many years. If you look around, you can probably see some of me right now. What am I?
Paint.

If there are four apples and you take away three, how many do you have?
You took three apples, so you have three.

Which month has 28 days?
All of them, of course!

What has a thumb and four fingers but is not alive?
A glove.

If snakes marry, what might their towels say?
Hissss and hers.

When you have me, you feel like sharing me. But if you share me, you don't have me. What am I?
A secret.

95

What does a cat have that a dog doesn't?

Kittens.

Two fathers and two sons sat down to eat eggs for breakfast. They ate exactly three eggs, and each person had an egg. Explain how they did it.

One of the fathers is also a grandfather. Therefore, one father is both a son and a father. That makes three people, so each got an egg.

How can a leopard change its spots?

By moving from one spot to another.

What weighs more, a pound of iron or a pound of feathers?

Both weigh the same. A pound is a pound.

My feet stay warm, but my head is cold. No one can move me, I'm just too old. What am I?

A mountain.

What has a horn but doesn't honk?

A rhinoceros.

What five-letter word becomes shorter when you add two letters to it?

Short.

What kind of coat can you put on only when it's wet?

A coat of paint.

What flies around all day but never goes anywhere?

A flag.

Dad Facts! Ted St. Martin holds the record for the most basketball free throws made in a row. He made 5,221 consecutive free throws in 1996.

What ship has two mates but no captain?

A relationship.

You can serve it, but you never eat it. What is it?

A tennis ball.

What small box can weigh over a hundred pounds?

A scale.

Why would a baby ant be confused when he looks at his family?

Because all his uncles are ants.

97

How do you spell "cow" in eleven letters?
SEE-O-DOUBLE-U.

What travels the world but stays in one spot?
A stamp.

What always sleeps with its shoes on?
A horse.

What is easy to lift but hard to throw?
A feather.

A taxi driver is going the wrong way down a one-way street. He passes four police officers, but none of them stop him. Why?
He is walking.

What seven letters did Sophie say when she saw the refrigerator had no food?
O-I-C-U-R-M-T.

What can you find in water that never gets wet?
A reflection.

What word contains 26 letters but only has three syllables?
"Alphabet."

Forward I am heavy, but backward I am not. What am I?
The word "ton."

What is at the end of everything?
The letter "g."

What comes down but never goes up?
Rain.

A little girl goes to the store and buys one dozen eggs. As she goes home, all but three break. How many eggs are left unbroken?
Three.

The more you take, the more you leave behind. What are they?
Footsteps.

What man cannot live in a house?

A snowman.

A man leaves home and turns left three times, only to return home facing two men wearing masks. Who are those two men?

A catcher and an umpire.

What four-letter word can be written forward, backward, or upside down and can still be read from left to right?

"NOON."

What can clap without any hands?

Thunder.

What word is pronounced the same if you take away four of its five letters?

"Queue."

I'm never thirsty but I always drink. What am I?

A fish.

You can break me without touching or seeing me. What am I?

A promise.

How can you cross a river without getting wet?

Walk across when it's frozen.

Dad Facts! Laughter is good for your mental and physical health. It reduces stress, enhances your mood, boosts the immune system, improves blood flow, and much more.

A dog was on a 24-foot chain and wanted a ball that was 26 feet away. How did the dog reach the ball?

The chain was not attached to anything.

The wise humans are sure of it. The fools know it. The rich want it. The greatest of heroes fear it, yet the lowliest of cowards would die for it. What is it?

Nothing.

I have a face and tail, but I am not alive. What am I?

A coin.

What's a 10-letter word that starts with G-A-S?

An automobile.

Zachary's parents have three sons. Snap, Crackle, and...?

Zachary!

A girl fell off a 20-foot ladder. She wasn't hurt. Why?

She fell from the bottom step.

If April showers bring May flowers, what do Mayflowers bring?

Pilgrims.

I am a bird, a fruit, and a person. What am I?

A Kiwi.

People make me, save me, change me, and raise me. What am I?

Money.

Where does success come before work?

The dictionary.

A word in this sentence is misspelled. What word is it?

"Misspelled."

You draw a line. Without touching it, how do you make it a longer line?

Draw a short line next to it, and now it's the longer line.

I am a word of letters three; add two and fewer there will be. What word am I?

"Few."

You walk into a room with a match, a kerosene lamp, a candle, and a fireplace. What do you light first?

The match.

If you drop me, I'm sure to crack, but give me a smile and I'll always smile back. What am I?

A mirror.

What breaks yet never falls, and what falls yet never breaks?

Day and night.

Almost everyone needs it, asks for it, and gives it, but almost nobody takes it. What is it?

Advice.

What starts with a "p," ends with an "e," and has thousands of letters?

The post office.

I appear when there is light, but if a light shines on me, I disappear. What am I?

A shadow.

If two's company and three's a crowd, what are four and five?

Nine.

What is cut on a table but is never eaten?

A deck of cards.

Dad Facts! There are more than 350,000 different types of beetles in the world. There are so many that beetles represent 25 percent of all animal species.

I have three letters in my name. Take away two letters and I sound the same. What am I?

A pea.

105

Stories You Can Tell... Are Jokes

Once Upon a Time for Jokes

Short jokes are great for quick laughs. But some jokes can't be rushed. These jokes, story jokes, draw listeners into the world of the joke. Settings, characters, and action work together to create excitement and build tension for the final punch line.

When a story begins, the storyteller has all the power. The audience doesn't know where the story is going. They wait for punch lines with increasing curiosity, which makes punch lines more satisfying. The best storytellers understand their audience and know how to immerse them deeper into a story, which is why dads make such good storytellers for their kids.

As you will find in this chapter, a story joke doesn't need to be serious. The characters can be as ridiculous as a pet penguin or a sarcastic farmer. The settings can be as silly as a deserted island or a hotel bathroom. The action might mislead you to increase tension, but the final destination is always a memorable punch line.

When you read these jokes, don't skip to the punch line. Enjoy the journey.

A mother walks into her son's room and says, "Wake up! You're gonna be late for school!" But the son pulls a blanket over his head and says, "I'm not going to school today." Surprised by her son's boldness, the mother asks, "And, why not?" The son says, "Two reasons: First, the students at school don't like me. And second, the teachers don't like me either." The mother says, "Well, I'll give you two reasons why you *are* going to school today." The son asks, "What are they?" The mother says, "First, you're 45 years old. And second, you're the principal!"

A man runs into a hospital emergency room screaming, "Help me! I'm shrinking!" A nurse grabs the man and sits him down in the waiting room. "We're very busy here today, sir. You're going to have to be a *little patient.*"

On Halloween night a boy knocks on a door and says, "Trick or treat?" A woman opens the door. Confused by the boy's appearance, she says, "I don't know if I can give you a treat. What are you supposed to be?" The boy answers, "A werewolf!" The woman shakes her head, unimpressed. "But you're not wearing a costume." The boy replies, "Well, it's not a full moon yet, is it?"

A man walks into a shop and sees a cute dog. He asks the shopkeeper, "Does your dog bite?" The shopkeeper says, "Never. She loves everybody." The man reaches down to pet the dog and the dog bites him. "Ouch!" the man says. "I thought you said your dog doesn't bite!" The shopkeeper replies, "That's not my dog."

A man dreams of being in the circus. When he finally works up the courage to tell a circus ringmaster, he explains, "I can do the best bird impression you have ever seen." The ringmaster says, "That's nothing special. A lot of people can do bird impressions." The disappointed man sighs and says, "Okay." Then he flaps his arms and flies away.

Three men are traveling through the desert. It's very hot and they are very thirsty. At the height of the day's heat, they come to a mysterious waterslide with these words written in gold: "Slide down and yell the drink of your choice. At the bottom, you will find a pool of that beverage." The three men are very excited. The first man slides down and yells, "Water!" and splashes into a cool pool of water. The next man goes down and yells, "Lemonade!" and splashes into a refreshing pool of lemonade. The final man goes down, and overwhelmed with excitement, yells, "Weeeee!"

A police officer pulls over a woman driving a truck full of penguins. The officer asks the woman, "What are you doing with all of these penguins?" "These are my penguins," the woman replies. "They belong to me." "You need to take them to the zoo," the police officer insists. The driver nods and says, "Will do." The next day, at the same time, and at the same intersection, the police officer sees the same truck filled with penguins. He pulls the woman over again and says, "I thought I told you to take these penguins to the zoo." The woman nods. "I did," she says calmly. "And today, I'm taking them to the movies."

A student nervously approaches his teacher. "Can I get in trouble for something I didn't do?" The teacher replies, "Of course not." "Great," the student says. "Because I didn't do my homework."

A mom sees her young daughter crying too hard to speak. So, she asks her son, "Why is your little sister crying?" The boy shrugs and replies, "Because I helped her." The mom relaxes and says, "But that's a good thing! What did you help her with?" The boy says, "I helped her eat the rest of her candy."

A teacher sees one of his students making ugly faces at other students on the playground. He stops to gently explain that's not nice behavior. Smiling kindly, the teacher says, "When I was a little boy, I was told that if I made ugly faces, my face would freeze like that." The mischievous student looks up and replies, "Well, you can't say you weren't warned."

Three friends are stranded on a desert island. One day, one of the friends digs a hole and, to his surprise, finds a lamp. "Maybe it's a magic lamp," shouts one of the men. "Rub it and see if a genie appears!" The man who found the lamp quickly rubs it and, to his astonishment, smoke pours out of the spout and curls around their heads. "Holy cow! That's a real genie," he cries. "Yes," a deep voice resounds. "I will grant you three wishes. Remember to use them wisely. There will only be three wishes allowed." One of the friends rushes forward and shouts, "I want to go home, now!" The genie snaps his fingers, and the first friend vanishes in a puff of purple smoke. "I want to go home, too," the second friend proclaims. In an instant, he, too, is gone. The third man looks at the empty island and the blue expanse of the sea. He hears nothing but the cry of the seagulls and the crash of the waves. He swallows a sob and says, "I sure am lonely. I wish I had my friends back."

A pirate walks into a bar with an eye patch, a peg leg, and a hook for a hand. The bartender notices his leg and asks, "How did you get that peg leg?" The pirate replies, "It were many years ago. I were walkin' on the deck when a wave swept a shark aboard. The shark bit off me leg!" "Wow," replies the bartender. "What about the hand?" The pirate nods. "It were many years ago. I were walkin' on the deck when a wave swept a killer whale aboard. The whale bit me bloomin' hand off!" "Oh no," says the bartender. "How about the eye?" The pirate replies, "It were many years ago. I were walkin' on the deck when a seagull came outta nowhere and pooped in me eye." "And that blinded you?" asked the bartender. "No, 'twas me first day with the hook."

A cruise ship passes by a remote island in the Pacific Ocean. The passengers cluster on the deck to see a bearded man running around and waving his arms wildly. "Captain," one passenger asks, "who is that man over there?" "I have no idea," the captain says, "but he goes nuts every year we pass him."

An old man went to the doctor complaining of an awful pain in his leg. "I'm afraid it's just old age," the doctor explained to the old man. "There's nothing we can do about it." The old man fumed. "That's impossible! You don't know what you are doing." The doctor countered, "How can you possibly know I'm wrong?" The old man replied, "Well, it's quite obvious. My other leg is just fine and it's the exact same age!"

A wife who knows her husband is feeling lonely on a business trip sends him a sweet message that reads, "If you're sleeping, send me your dreams. If you're laughing, send me your smile. If you're eating, send me a bite. If you're drinking, send me a sip. If you're crying, send me your tears. I love you!" With his first smile in days, the husband replies, "I'm on the toilet. Please advise."

A man close to dying goes to his lawyer and says, "I need to make a will, but I don't know how to do it." The lawyer smiles and says, "Don't worry, leave it all to me." The man, quite upset, says, "Well, I figured you would take a big portion, but what about my wife and kids?"

A linguistics professor is lecturing his class. "In English," he says, "a double negative forms a positive. However, in some languages, such as Russian, a double negative remains a negative. But there isn't a single language, not one, in which a double positive can express a negative." The class nods in agreement, all except a student in the back of the room who says, "Yeah, right."

A man walks into a psychiatrist's office and says to the doctor, "I've got no money, I've got no job, and I don't know how to cope with the stress of it all." The psychiatrist says, "I understand. We've all got problems. You'll need several years of treatment at $75/hour." The man looks at the psychiatrist and says, "Well, that solves your problems. What about mine?"

A burglar breaks into a house late at night. While he is taking valuables, he hears a voice: "Jesus is watching." The burglar glances around the room, but he can't figure out where the voice is coming from. Then, he hears the voice again: "Jesus is watching." The burglar looks around some more and notices there's a parrot. He asks the parrot, "Was that you talking?" The parrot says, "Yes." The burglar asks, "Who names a parrot Jesus?" The parrot says, "My name is Moses. Jesus is the pit bull."

A man approaches the desk clerk at a prominent hotel. "Excuse me," he says. "Is there a woman staying here with one eye named Jennifer Thomas?" The clerk says, "I don't know. What's the name of her other eye?"

A park ranger tells a group of hikers worried about bears that black bears are usually not dangerous. He even gives the hikers a few bells to put on their backpacks. He tells them the black bears will hear the bells and stay away. However, the park ranger says that grizzly bears are extremely dangerous. He warns the hikers, "If you see any grizzly bear footprints or poop, leave the area immediately." "How do we recognize grizzly bear poop?" asks one of the hikers. "Easy," says the park ranger. "It's full of bells."

A man asks God, "Is it true that to you a billion years is like a second?" God replies, "Yes." Amazed that he got a response, the man asks another question, "God, is it true that to you a billion dollars is like a penny?" God says, "Yes." Encouraged by the conversation, the man asks, "God, can I have a billion dollars?" God says, "Sure, just a second."

A man named Henry bought an old horse from a farmer for $250. The farmer agreed to deliver the horse to Henry the next day. But the next day, the farmer showed up at Henry's house with bad news. "I'm sorry," said the farmer. "The horse died overnight." Henry replied, "That's too bad. I'll just take my money back." The farmer said, "Unfortunately, that's not possible. I already spent your money." Henry didn't lose his temper. He said, "Alright, just bring me the dead horse." Surprised, the farmer asked, "Why? What are you gonna do with a dead horse?" Henry replied, "I'm going to raffle him off." The farmer laughed and said, "You can't raffle off a dead horse. Who'd buy a ticket?" Henry answered, "Sure I can, just watch me. I won't tell anybody the horse is dead." A month later, the farmer saw Henry and asked, "What happened with that dead horse? Did you raffle him off?" Henry said, "I sure did. I sold 500 tickets at $5 per ticket." The farmer said, "Didn't anyone complain?" Henry said, "Just the guy who won. So I gave him his $5 back."

A man goes to his doctor and says, "Doc, I'm worried my wife is losing her hearing." The doctor says, "Well, there's a simple test you can do to be sure. All you need to do is stand 40 feet away from her and, in a normal voice, ask her a simple question, and see if she can hear you. If not, try again at 30 feet, 20 feet, and so on until you know how far it takes for her to hear you." That night, the man decides to do the test. While his wife is cooking dinner, he stands in the living room 40 feet away from her and asks, "Honey, what are we having for dinner?" No response. So he moves 10 feet closer. "Honey, what are we having for dinner?" No response again. Again he moves closer and asks, "What are we having for dinner?" Still, no response. He goes all the way into the kitchen and asks, "Honey, what are we having for dinner?" And yet again, no response. Finally, he walks right behind his wife and asks slowly, "What are we having for dinner?" She turns around and says, "For the fifth time, Harry, we're having chicken!"

A woman in labor suddenly shouts, "Wouldn't! Couldn't! Shouldn't! Can't!" A doctor looks the woman calmly in the eye and says, "Don't worry, ma'am. Those are just contractions."

A struggling artist visits a studio where his paintings are for sale. The studio owner says, "I've got some good news for you and some bad news. The good news is that somebody bought all of your paintings. All I needed to do was tell him that artwork goes up in value whenever the artist passes away." "Well, that's great," says the artist. "I'm rich. What's the bad news?" The studio owner says, "The buyer is your doctor."

Following a heated argument, a man and his wife are driving down a country road, not saying a word. As they pass a field of donkeys, goats, and pigs, the husband sarcastically asks, "Relatives of yours?" "Yep," the wife replies. "My in-laws."

A young boy enters a barber shop. The barber sees him and whispers to a customer, "This is the dumbest kid in the world. Watch, I'll prove it to you." The barber puts a dollar bill in one hand and two quarters in his other hand. Then he calls the boy over and asks, "Which do you want, son?" The boy doesn't think about it. He takes the quarters and leaves. "What did I tell you?" says the barber. "That kid never learns!" Later, when the customer leaves, he sees the same young boy coming out of an ice cream parlor. "Hey, son! May I ask you a question? Why did you take the quarters instead of the dollar bill?" The boy licks his ice cream cone and replies, "Because as soon as I take the dollar, the game is over!"

A man driving by a farm sees a beautiful horse that he wants to buy. He pulls over and finds the owner, but the owner says, "Are you sure? This horse is very strange. It only recognizes two commands. When you want to go, you say 'Thank Goodness,' and when you want to stop, you say 'Banana.'" The man agrees it's strange, but it isn't a dealbreaker. He says, "Let me try riding him. If it goes well, I'll buy the horse for $10,000." The owner agrees, so the man gets on the horse and says, "Thank Goodness." Sure enough, the horse takes off running, faster than any horse the man has ever ridden. But, after a few minutes of fun riding, the man wants to stop. But he can't remember the word he's supposed to say to make the horse stop. "Blueberries," he tries. The horse keeps running. "Broccoli! Brownies!" The horse still doesn't stop. "Brakes, please!" The man tries everything that comes to mind. But nothing works. Worst of all, the horse is heading straight for a cliff. Time is running out. Finally, the man yells, "Bananas!" and the horse stops, inches from the edge of the cliff. The man lets out a deep breath, wipes his brow, and says, "Thank Goodness."

127

After running over a rooster that was crossing the road, a driver stops his car at a nearby farmhouse to see if he can find the rooster's owner. When the farmer answers the door, the driver says, "I'm very sorry. I ran over your rooster. But I want you to know that I'm prepared to replace him." "Okay," says the farmer, "But let's hear how well you crow first."

Two hunters named Smith and Davis save up their money to go on a safari in Africa. On the first day they get into a big argument about who is a better hunter. The argument ends with Smith betting Davis $100 that he'll be the first to shoot a lion. "In fact," says Smith, "I'm going to go hunt a lion right now." So, Smith loads his rifle, heads out of camp, and goes to find a lion. About an hour later, a lion pokes his head into Davis's tent. The lion says, "You know a guy named Smith?" Trembling, Davis says, "Yes." The lion says, "Well, he owes you $100."

A new dad hurries out of a restaurant with his crying baby. He walks around patting his baby's back, saying, "Easy, Oliver, it's going to be alright. Relax, you're okay, Oliver. You're gonna be fine." A woman walking by sees the man struggling with his baby. She wants to encourage him, so she approaches the man and says, "You're a good dad. Little Oliver there is lucky to have you." The man looks at her confused and says, "Thanks, but the baby's name isn't Oliver. I'm Oliver!"

Three sons grow up to be very wealthy businessmen. So, for their mom's 75th birthday, they each buy a very expensive birthday gift. The first son brags that he bought their mom a $400,000 house. The second son brags that he bought their mom a $500,000 sports car. The third son brags that he bought their mom a parrot that can recite 100 classic books because their mom's eyesight is too poor to read anymore. He also brags that the one-of-a-kind bird took five years to train and cost him $1 million. A few days later, their mom writes each son a letter. To the first son she writes, "Thank you, but the house is too large. I only use one room." To the second son, she writes, "Thank you, but the car is unnecessary. I never leave the house." And to the third son, she writes, "Thank you for being the only son who truly knows what I like. The chicken was delicious!"

Just for Kids: The Next Generation of Comedians

Dad Jokes versus Kid Jokes

Congratulations, you've read more than 750 dad jokes! That's a lot of jokes. But there's still room for more.

Dads, moms, and other adults, you can skip to the end of the chapter. Jokes will appear there soon. The next part is just for kids—our next generation of comedians.

* * * KIDS ONLY * * *

Kids (and adults who don't follow directions), let's be honest, some dad jokes are better than others. We try our best, but dads can't resist telling a few jokes that get bigger eye rolls than belly laughs. And that's okay. Everybody has their own unique sense of humor.

The truth is, nobody understands what makes kids laugh better than kids. That means the best person to write new jokes for kids is YOU! At the beginning of this book, I challenged you to continue the tradition of telling dad jokes by creating your own variations. Well, why wait? Let's get your comedy career started today!

If you can write a dad joke, you can write a kid joke; knock, knock joke; or any other kind of joke. The fundamentals of writing comedy are the same, regardless of style. The following pages include ten "fun-damental" tips for writing comedy with space to write down your own ideas for jokes. This part of the book is just for you. No idea is too silly or strange.

Afterward, write down your finished jokes and share them with your friends and family. Soon you'll be getting bigger laughs than the funniest dad you know.

Good luck!

Comedy Writing Tip #1: Be observant.

The world is full of topics for jokes: school, relationships, food, travel, animals, etc. Wherever you go, pay attention to what makes you laugh. Pay attention to what others are laughing about, too. Professional comedians always write these things down and think about what makes them funny, so keep a notebook handy for recording your thoughts.

In addition to things that make you laugh, think about what makes you frustrated, angry, or embarrassed. Some of the best comedy comes from bad days. You will be surprised how many people feel the same way. If you can turn those moments into comedy, it will help you and others feel better about bad days.

What are some funny observations you've had recently?

135

Comedy Writing Tip #2: Focus on a punch line.

Once you've identified a funny topic, you need a punch line. Punch lines are the big finish and funniest part of a joke. There are many ways to write a punch line, but it's best to keep it short and unexpected.

What's your favorite punch line? Why is it so effective?

Comedy Writing Tip #3: Keep your setup simple.

Since the punch line is the funniest part of a joke, don't make your setup too long or confusing. Cut out any unnecessary words. Get to the punch line as fast as possible. Then, start a new joke.

Pick a joke you think is too long, maybe even one from this book. Write a shorter setup for it here:

Comedy Writing Tip #4: Be silly. Exaggerate reality.

Jokes aren't facts. It's okay to stretch the truth. In fact, it's funnier when you exaggerate details. Something bigger than a house, older than a dinosaur, or slower than grass growing is funnier than the real size, age, or speed of something. Jokes are meant to be silly, so be as silly as possible.

Pick something you see or do and write down as many exaggerated descriptions of it as you can:

....

....

....

....

....

....

....

Comedy Writing Tip #5: Be unexpected.

The best jokes have surprise endings. That means you need to lead your audience in the wrong direction before delivering a punch line. Convince your audience you are going in one direction and reverse it at the very end. But don't confuse them. The punch line needs to make sense. And don't forget: Keep the setup short and simple.

Think about something funny that surprised you. What was it? Why was it so funny?

Comedy Writing Tip #6: Use wordplay.

Many of the jokes in this book rely on puns, which are a type of wordplay. Puns take words that sound alike and create surprising punch lines by using the unexpected meaning of a word. Try using puns or twisting word assumptions to deliver unexpected punch lines in your jokes.

Choose some of your favorite puns from this book. Try writing new jokes with them. For a bigger challenge, make a list of different puns and turn them into jokes, too.

141

Comedy Writing Tip #7: Experiment with joke structures and style.

Jokes come in many sizes and structures. As long as you have a setup and a punch line, you have a joke. After writing question-and-answer jokes, try writing one-liners or knock, knock jokes. As you improve, try writing longer jokes in the form of a story.

Afterward, try doing impressions and telling jokes with funny facial expressions. Find your favorite style. You can even create a brand-new joke structure. There are no limitations. If you develop a unique style, it will help you stand out from other joke writers and comedians.

What's your favorite style of joke? Try writing a few jokes in that style.

143

Comedy Writing Tip #8: Be brave. Test your jokes.

The first time you tell a new joke, it's possible nobody laughs. That's normal. Failing is part of the creative process. You must be brave. Don't give up. Make adjustments and try again. The best comedians in the world tell the same joke again and again until they've figured out how to get the biggest laughs possible.

Be brave and tell five of your own jokes in front of friends or family. Then, write about it here. Try it again on a different day and see how much you've improved. Keep repeating this process until you are happy with the laughs you get.

145

Comedy Writing Tip #9: Improve your timing.

The best joke tellers have great timing. That means they know how to speed up or slow down a joke before delivering a punch line at the perfect time. Great timing takes lots of testing. Once you have a punch line that gets laughs, test how long you can wait silently before delivering your punch line.

As you wait, watch your audience. Let the tension build. You will be surprised by how the pacing of a joke from start to finish can change the number of laughs you get.

Write down the names of some of your favorite comedians or people who make you laugh. What makes their timing and delivery better than that of other joke tellers?

147

Comedy Writing Tip #10: Have fun!

Writing jokes is meant to be fun. It takes work, practice, and courage to continue. But never forget to have fun. If an audience sees you having fun, they will have fun, too.

What's the most fun part about telling jokes to people?

Ideas for New Jokes

On the following pages, think about the comedy tips you've learned and write down the things, moments, and feelings you find funny.

What's funny about food?

....

....

What's funny about traveling?

....

....

What's funny about animals?

....

....

What's funny about technology?

· ·

· ·

What's funny about sports/hobbies?

· ·

· ·

What's funny about your daily routine?

· ·

· ·

What else do you find funny?

· ·

· ·

150

What Is the Punch Line?

Funny ideas are great for a joke setup, but you don't have a complete joke without an ending. Now is the time to finish your jokes with funny punch lines.

Pick out your best ideas. Make them relatable. Combine them with other funny ideas. Lead your audience in one direction and surprise them with a funny ending. Finally, write down your jokes in the following pages for everybody to read.

Good luck!

Comedy Glossary

Bit: A small part of a larger comedy routine that focuses on a joke, story, or idea.

Callback: A joke that refers to an earlier joke or moment, connecting ideas for a bigger laugh.

Catchphrase: A memorable and distinct phrase associated with a person, character, or group that repeats it often.

Dry Humor or Deadpan: Humor delivered without emotion, using a serious delivery and straight face to create a funny contrast with the joke topic.

Heckler: Someone who disrupts a performance with unwelcome and distracting comments.

Improvisation or Improv: Comedy performed without a plan that relies on quick thinking, creativity, and flexibility to adapt as the performance continues.

Irony: Communicating something that is the opposite of what's being said or done, usually for comedic effect.

Observational Comedy: Relatable humor about the parts of everyday life that people often overlook.

One-Liner: A short joke or remark in one sentence or less.

Parody: A form of satire that copies a style, work, or genre in a funny or mocking way.

Physical Comedy: Comedy that uses action, gestures, and body language.

Punch Line: The last part of a joke or story that delivers the big laugh.

Puns: A form of wordplay that uses multiple meanings or sounds of a word in a funny way.

Sarcasm: Using irony to make fun of something and/or show annoyance about something. It is typically done in a tone of voice that makes the sarcastic intent obvious.

Satire: Using humor, irony, or exaggeration to criticize or make fun of something, often to highlight a problem and encourage change.

Self-Deprecation: When someone uses humor to make fun of themselves.

Setup: The beginning of a joke that sets up and leads to the punch line.

Stand-Up Comedy: When a comedian performs a set of jokes for an audience, usually on a stage.

Timing: The skill of delivering a joke at a speed and rhythm that maximizes the potential of the joke.

Author Bio

CHRIS CATE is a professional author and unprofessional biography writer. His books are worldwide bestsellers and literary masterpieces according to his wife, three kids, and dog that thinks it's a kid. He pays for their food, shelter, and affection in Nashville, TN, where they live mostly on a soccer field. His publisher wants him to mention his work as a high school teacher, college professor, news reporter, spokesperson, comedian, and parenting influencer. His recent books include *How to Make a Unicorn Laugh* and *How to Make a Ninja Laugh*. His recent biographies include this one.